BIRMINGHAM

by J.P. Lethbridge

Dedicated to my Parents

Birmingham Citizens have shown courage in many places ranging from the fighting in the deserts of North Africa during the Second World War to saving life in the City's factories after industrial accidents. This book celebrates the lives and deeds of such heroes.

Contents

Introduction..3

The Victoria Cross...4

Private Sims, Private Cooper, Private Wassall, Private Ravenhill,
Sergeant Parker, Lieutenant James, Private Vickers, Private Turrall,
Sergeant Gill, Sergeant Knight, Sergeant Finch, Lance Corporal Onions,
Private Colley, Lance Corporal Wilcox, Lance Corporal Amey,
Lieutenant Colonel Marshall, Captain Waters, Able Seaman Savage,
Lieutenant Colonel Foote, Lance Corporal Kenneally.

The George Cross...29

Private Miller, Flying Officer Graveley, Lieutenant Reynolds,
Acting Squadron.Leader Moxey, Section Commander Inwood,
Station Officer Mosedale, William Waterson, Charles Wilcox.

Other heroes..39

Captain Gough DSO, Corporal Allbut DCM, The Forbes Brothers,
Colonel Innes, Councillor Henry Lynn Shaw, Henri Chatelain,
My Grandfather.

Introduction

Birmingham men have fought in Britain's foreign and civil wars since the beginning of the town's recorded history. For instance it is recorded that one of the De Birmingham family who owned the town in the middle ages took part in the hundred years war and fought at Crecy and Poiters. Doubtless earlier unrecorded Brummies fought in other wars such as Alfred's defence of England against the Vikings.

In addition Birmingham has on occasion itself been the scene of fighting. In particular it was the scene of a fierce battle during the Civil War.

However it has not been until recent times that gallantry awards have existed or that newspapers have existed which have been interested in recording the courage that soldiers have always shown in battle. Britain's most distinguished gallantry award the Victoria Cross was started in 1856 during the Crimean War. The other gallantry awards such as the Military Cross and the Military Medal are all more recent creations.

Many men show courage and do not win medals. For modern times their stories can be obtained from the back files of local newspapers. However local newspapers that take an interest in the doings of ordinary people were themselves a Victorian invention.

Courage can be displayed by civilians as well as soldiers. Policemen and firemen are expected to be brave as much as servicemen are. Courage is also needed on occasion by factory workers who are dealing with industrial accidents. Finally even the most ordinary person living the most routine life may suddenly have to show courage say in an accident. However it has not been until this century that such courage has been awarded with medals. Because of the above considerations this book's earliest hero won a VC in 1856. The book then looks at other Birmingham VC winners; looks at those Brummies who have won the G.C; and then takes a look at winners of other awards. It concludes by taking a look at some of those brave men who never won medals, such as my grandfather who marched away in 1914 a healthy teenager looking forward to having some adventure and to seeing the world and who returned in 1919 broken in health at the age of 24.

Women are as brave as men but until very recent times they were not allowed to take part in combat and they were normally banned from taking part in the more dangerous peacetime occupations. Some women won the George Cross during the second World War but none of them came from Birmingham.

It should however be said that until modern times every woman who had a child was risking both extreme pain and a chance of dying in childbirth that was comparable to the risks that a soldier faced as he went over the top in the First World War. If it was not for the courage that woman have shown down the ages there would be no human race.

The Victoria Cross

The Victoria Cross was founded by Royal Warrant on the 29th of January 1856 during the Crimean War. The first awards were made to men who had displayed gallantry earlier during that war including one of the men featured in this book.

The Victoria Cross can only be awarded for courage displayed in the face of the enemy. Such courage may take the form of a single supreme act of heroism such as standing up in No Man's Land in the First World War in broad daylight under machine gun and sniper fire to cut a barbed wire fence that is holding up the progress of an attack; or it can consist of a series of acts of heroism displayed on one day or over a period of days; or it can take the form of heroic leadership of a unit in the face of the enemy.

The VC consists of a Maltese Cross ensigned with the Royal Crest and a scroll inscribed "For Valour". It is linked by a V shaped link to a bar engraved on the front with laurel leaves and on the back with the name of the medal winner. It is worn on the left side of the chest and is suspended from a 1½ inch wide red ribbon. Before 1920 the VC ribbon was dark red for the army and blue for the navy but since then it has been the same colour for all services.

Birmingham's VC winners have ranged in rank from privates to Lieutenant Colonels. Several were awarded posthumously to men who died that others might live. They came from all walks of life ranging from army officer's sons to men who were born and bred in the back to back houses of inner city Birmingham. All were united by one thing. That is they displayed supreme courage in the face of the enemy.

Private Sims

Full Name and Unit: Private John Joseph Sims, the 1st Battalion, the 34th Regiment (this unit later became the Border Regiment).

Background: John Sims was born in the Bloomsbury area of London in February 1836. In the mid nineteenth century army units were known by number not name. Some had regional connections but these were not very strong. Private Sims served in the army during the Crimean war. In this war Britain, France and Turkey fought against the Tsarist Russians to stop them from overrunning the Turkish Empire.

Deed: "For having on the 18th of June 1855 after the Regiment had retired into the trenches from the assault on the Redan gone out into the open ground under a heavy fire in broad daylight and brought in wounded soldiers from outside the trenches".

Private Sims was among the earliest men to be awarded the VC.

Subsequent Career: Private Sims died in Birmingham on the 14th of September 1881 at the age of 45. In the nineteenth century average life expectancy was much lower than it is today particularly for ordinary people.

Private Cooper

Full name and regiment: Private James Cooper 2nd Battalion the 24th Regiment (this unit later became the South Wales Borderers).

Background: James Cooper was born in Birmingham on the 5th of February 1840.

Deed: The Andaman islands are located in the Bay of Bengal. In the mid nineteenth century they had a bad reputation. Over the centuries they had often been attacked by pirates and slavers coming out from India and Indo China and as a result the native tribal

Regiment.	Rank and Name.	Act of Bravery for which recommended.
9th Regiment	No. 1051 Private John Lyons	For, on the 10th June, 1855, taking up a live shell which fell among the guard of the trenches, and throwing it over the parapet.
23rd Regiment	Brevet Lieutenant-Colonel Edward W. D. Bell	Recommended for his gallantry, more particularly at the Battle of the Alma, where he was the first to seize upon and capture one of the enemy's guns, which was limbered up, and being carried off. He, moreover, succeeded to the command of that gallant Regiment which he brought out of action ; all his Senior Officers having been killed or wounded.
23rd Regiment	Lieutenant Luke O'Connor..	Was one of the centre Serjeants at the Battle of the Alma, and advanced between the Officers, carrying the colours. When near the redoubt, Lieutenant Anstruther, who was carrying a colour, was mortally wounded, and he was shot in the breast at the same time, and fell ; but, recovering himself, snatched up the colour from the ground, and continued to carry it till the end of the action, although urged by Captain Granville to relinquish it, and go to the rear, on account of his wound ; was recommended for, and received his commission for his services at the Alma. Also behaved with great gallantry at the assault on the Redan, 8th September, 1855, where he was shot through both thighs.
23rd Regiment	No. 2945 Corporal Robert Shields	For volunteering, on the 8th of September, 1855, to go out to the front from the 5th parallel, after the attack on the Redan, to bring in Lieutenant Dyneley, who was wounded, and found afterwards to be mortally so.
34th Regiment	No. 3837 Private William Coffey	For having, on the 29th March, 1855, thrown a lighted shell, that fell into the trench over the parapet.
34th Regiment	No. 3482 Private John J. Sims	For having, on the 18th June, 1855, after the Regiment had retired into the trenches from the assault on the Redan, gone out into the open ground, under a heavy fire, in broad daylight, and brought in wounded soldiers outside the trenches.
41st Regiment	Brevet-Major Hugh Rowland-	For rescuing Colonel Haly, of the 47th Regiment, from Russian soldiers, Colonel Haly having been wounded and surrounded by them, and for gallant exertions in holding the ground occupied by his advanced picquet against the enemy, at the commencement of the Battle of Inkerman.

✻

6

population came to have an intense hostility for all outsiders, often with tragic results for shipwrecked trading vessels. The Andamanese did not ask questions as to what their business was and in any case it was not unknown for legitimate trading ships to dabble in slaving.

In April 1867 a trading ship the "Assam Valley" foundered off the island of Little Andaman with the loss of her skipper and seven crew. A punitive expedition which consisted of H.M S. Arracan and a 100 men of the 2nd 24th Battalion was sent to find out what had happened.

A 17 man force was landed. As they landed their boat sank but nevertheless the shore party managed to find the bodies of the crew of the "Assam Valley" and to kill several dozen Andamanese islanders who attempted to attack the landing party.

The shore party then had to be rescued in its turn.This rescue had to be performed by a small boat which was commanded by ship's Assistant Surgeon Douglas and manned by Privates Bell, Cooper, Griffiths and Murphy. It took three perilous trips through high surf and under hostile arrow fire to get the shore party to safety and the boat's entire crew of five men were each awarded the VC.

To quote the "London Gazette" of the 17th December 1867:

"The four privates behaved in a cool and collected manner rowing through the roughest surf when the slightest hesitation or want of pluck on the part of any one of them would have been attended by the gravest results".

Later life: Private Cooper died in Birmingham on the 9th of August 1889. He was 49.

Afterword: the Bay of Bengal is notorious for piracy even today.

Private Wassall

Full Name and Unit: Private Samuel Wassall, the 2nd Battalion, the 80th Regiment (this unit later became the South Staffordshire Regiment).

Background: Private Wassall was born in Aston which was then

7

actually part of our city but legally still a Warwickshire village on the 28th July 1856. He won his VC in the Zulu wars.

Deed: "For his gallant conduct on having at the imminent risk of his own life saved that of Private Westwood of the same regiment.

On the 22nd January, 1879, when the camp at Isandhlwana was taken by the enemy Private Wassall retreated towards the Buffalo River in which he saw a comrade struggling and apparently drowning. He rode to the bank, dismounted, leaving his horse on the Zulu side rescued the man from the stream and again mounted his horse, dragging Private Westwood across the stream under a heavy shower of bullets".

Private Samuel Wassall died in Barrow in Furness in Lancashire on the 31st of January 1927. His VC was purchased by retired officers from his regiment and given to the Staffordshire Regiment's museum in Lichfield.

Private Ravenhill

Full Name and Unit: Private George Albert Ravenhill, 2nd Battalion, The Royal Scots Fusiliers.

Background: Private Ravenhill was born on the 23rd of February 1872 in Thimble Mill Lane in Aston, Birmingham. This lane runs alongside the Birmingham and Fazeley Canal. He was the son of Thomas and Mary-Anne Ravenhill and his father was a wood turner by trade. He won his VC in the Boer War.

Deed: "At Colenso, on the 15th December 1899, Private Ravenhill went several times under a heavy fire from his sheltered position as one of the escort to the guns to assist the officers and drivers who were trying to withdraw the guns of the 14th and 66th batteries, Royal Field Artillery, when the detachments serving them had all been killed, wounded or driven from them by infantry fire at close range, and helped to limber up one of the guns that were saved".

Subsequent Career: Private Ravenhill died in Birmingham of a heart attack on the 14th April 1921 aged 49. At the time of his death he was an army pensioner and was living at a back to back house behind Long Acre in Aston within a few hundred yards of the place where he was born. He left behind a widow Florence.

Sergeant Parker

Full Name and Unit: Sergeant Charles Edward Parker, Q Battery Royal Horse Artillery.

Background: Sergeant Parker was born in Birmingham on the 11th of March 1870 and he was the son of a veteran of the Crimean War. Young Charles Parker was educated at Bishop Ryder's School and joined the army as a trumpeter in 1884 at the age of fourteen.

Deed: During the Boer War: "On the occasion of the action at Korn Spruit on the 31st of March 1900, a British force including two batteries of the Royal Horse Artillery was retiring from Thabanchu towards Bloemfontein. The enemy had formed an ambush at Korn Spruit and before their presence was discovered by the main body had captured the greater portion of the baggage column and five out of the six guns of the leading battery.

When the alarm was given Q Battery, Royal Horse Artillery was within 300 yards of the Spruit. Major Phipps-Hornby, who commanded it at once wheeled about and moved off at a gallop under a very heavy fire. One gun upset when a wheel horse was shot and had to be abandoned, together with a wagon the horses of which were killed. The remainder of the battery reached a position close to some unfinished railway buildings and came into action 1,150 yards from the Spruit, remaining in action until ordered to retire. When the order to retire was received Major Phipps-Hornby ordered the guns and their limbers to be run back by hand to where the teams of uninjured horses stood behind the unfinished buildings. The few remaining gunners, assisted by a number of officers and men of a party of mounted infantry, and directed by Major Phipps-Hornby and Captain Humphreys, the only remaining officers of the battery, succeeded in running back four of the guns under shelter. One or two of the limbers were similarly withdrawn by hand but the work was most severe and the distance considerable. In consequence all concerned were so exhausted that they were unable to drag in the remaining limbers or the fifth gun. It now became necessary to risk the horses and volunteers were called for from among the drivers who readily responded. Several horses were killed and men wounded but at length only one gun and one limber were left exposed. Four separate attempts were made to rescue these but when no more horses were available the attempt had to be given up and the gun and limber were abandoned.

Meanwhile the other guns had been sent on one at a time and after passing within 700 or 800 yards of the enemy in rounding the head of the donga and crossing two spruits they eventually reached a place of safety where the battery was reformed.

After full consideration of the circumstances of the case the Field Marshal Commanding-in Chief in South Africa formed the opinion that the conduct of all ranks of Q Battery, Royal Horse Artillery, was conspiciously gallant and daring but that all were equally brave and devoted in their behaviour. He therefore decided to treat the case of the battery as one of collective gallantry under Rule 13 of the Victoria Cross Warrant and directed that one officer should be selected for the decoration of the Victoria Cross by the officers, one non-commissioned officer by the non-commissioned officers and two gunners or drivers by the gunners and drivers.

A difficulty arose with regards to the officer owing to the fact that there were only two unwounded officers - Major Phipps-Hornby and Captain Humphreys - available for the work of saving the guns and both of these had been conspicious by their gallantry and by the fearless manner in which they exposed themselves and each of them nominated the other for the decoration. It was ultimately decided in favour of Major Phipps-Hornby as having been the senior concerned".

The non-commissioned officers elected Sergeant Parker to be given the VC. The gunners and drivers voted for Gunner Isaac Lodge and Driver Henry Glassock.

Subsequent Career: Sergeant Parker was promoted to Battery Sergeant-Major. On his return to Birmingham he was given a civic reception and exchanged photographs with the then Lord Mayor who was Alderman Edwards.

Although he was 44 when World War One broke out Sergeant-Major Parker immediately volunteered again. He was wounded at the Battle of Loos in 1915 and was eventually discharged from the army because of heart trouble. He died in Coventry on the 9th of August 1918 at the age of 48 and is buried in Coventry's London Road Cemetary.

Lieutenant James

Full Name and Unit: 2nd Lieutenant Herbert James, the 4th Battalion, the Worcestershire Regiment.

Background: Lieutenant James was born in Ladywood, on the 13th of November 1888. His father was a master engraver whose premises were located in Warstone Lane. The young Herbert James was educated at Smethwick Central School and became a teacher at first Bearwood Road and then Brasshouse Lane School.

In 1909 Herbert James got fed up with teaching and joined the 21st Lancers as a private soldier. He served in Egypt and India and studied various languages on one occasion winning a £100 prize for his linguistic talents. By 1914 he had been promoted to lance corporal.

After the outbreak of war Lance Corporal James was promoted to Lieutenant and was transferred to the 4th Worcestershires.

Deed: "For most conspicious bravery during the operations in the southern zone of the Gallipoli peninsula.

On the 28th June 1915 when a portion of a regiment had been checked owing to all the officers being put out of action Second Lieutenant James who belonged to a neighbouring unit, entirely on his own initiative gathered together a body of men and led them forward under heavy shell and rifle fire. He then returned, organised a second party and again advanced. His gallant example put fresh life into the attack.

On the 3rd July in the same locality Second Lieutenant James headed a party of bomb throwers up a Turkish communications trench and after nearly all his bomb throwers had been killed or wounded he remained alone at the head of the trench and kept back the enemy single handed till a barrier had been built behind him and the trench secured. He was throughout exposed to a murderous fire".

Subsequent Career: Lieutenant James later fought in the Battle of the Somme and was wounded there. He eventually reached the rank of Major. He died in hospital in London on the 15th August 1958 at the age of seventy.

A funeral service for Major James was held at St Mary Abbot's church in Kensington in London on the 20th of August 1958. Among the mourners were General Sir Richard Gale who was the Colonel of the Worcestershire Regiment and other military representatives.

example had led on his party to make further efforts, which resulted in the recapture of the trench.

On the night of 18th-19th June, 1915, Captain O'Sullivan saved a critical situation in the same locality by his great personal gallantry and good leading.

Second Lieutenant George Arthur Boyd Rochfort, Special Reserve, 1st Battalion, Scots Guards.

For most conspicuous bravery in the trenches between Cambrin and La Bassée on 3rd August, 1915.

At 2 a.m. a German trench mortar bomb landed on the side of the parapet of the communication trench in which he stood, close to a small working party of his Battalion. He might easily have stepped back a few yards round the corner into perfect safety, but, shouting to his men to look out, he rushed at the bomb, seized it and hurled it over the parapet, where it at once exploded.

There is no doubt that this splendid combination of presence of mind and courage saved the lives of many of the working party.

Second Lieutenant Herbert James, 4th Battalion, The Worcestershire Regiment.

For most conspicuous bravery during the operations in the Southern Zone of the Gallipoli Peninsula.

On the 28th June, 1915, when a portion of a Regiment had been checked owing to all the Officers being put out of action, Second Lieutenant James, who belonged to a neighbouring unit, entirely on his own initiative gathered together a body of men and led them forward under heavy shell and rifle fire. He then returned, organised a second party, and again advanced. His gallant example put fresh life into the attack. On the 3rd July, in the same locality, Second Lieutenant James headed a party of bomb throwers up a Turkish communication trench, and, after nearly all his bomb throwers had been killed or wounded, he remained alone at the head of the trench and kept back the enemy single-handed till a barrier had been built behind him and the trench secured. He was throughout exposed to a murderous fire.

No. 10512 Serjeant James Somers, 1st Battalion, The Royal Inniskilling Fusiliers.

For most conspicuous bravery on the night of 1st-2nd July, 1915, in the Southern Zone

War Office,
1st September, 1915.

REGULAR FORCES.

COMMANDS AND STAFF.

The undermentioned appointments are made:—

PERSONAL STAFF.

Aide-de-Camp—

Lieutenant Sir Richard V. Sutton, Bt., 1st Life Guards, and to be seconded. Dated 24th August, 1915.

GENERAL STAFF.

General Staff Officers—

1st Grade—

Dated 24th August, 1915.

Major Hanway R. Cumming, The Durham Light Infantry, from the 2nd Grade, and to be temporary Lieutenant-Colonel whilst so employed.

Major Francis W. Gosset, D.S.O., Royal Artillery, from the 2nd Grade, and to be temporary Lieutenant-Colonel whilst so employed.

Lieutenant-Colonel Robert N. Greathed, Royal Artillery. Dated 25th August, 1915.

3rd Grade—

Captain Charles H. Edwards, The Royal Welsh Fusiliers, and to be seconded. Dated 24th August, 1915.

ADJUTANT-GENERAL'S AND QUARTERMASTER-GENERAL'S STAFF.

Deputy Assistant Adjutant and Quartermaster-Generals—

Captain Douglas C. Owen, The Duke of Cambridge's Own (Middlesex Regiment), and to be seconded. Dated 22nd August, 1915.

Captain Robert Q. Craufurd, The Royal Scots Fusiliers, in succession to Major H. W. Grubb, The Border Regiment. Dated 25th August, 1915.

ATTACHED TO HEADQUARTER UNITS.

Staff Captains—

Major G. Evans, from Superintendent, Remount Squadron, vice Captain W. J. J. S. Haskett-Smith, The Royal Irish Rifles. Dated 6th July, 1915.

Temporary Lieutenant W. W. Fox, The York and Lancaster Regiment, vice tempo-

Private Vickers

Full Name and Unit: Private Arthur Vickers, 2nd Battalion the Royal Warwickshire Regiment.

Background: Private Vickers was born on the 2nd of February 1882 in a courtyard house at the back of Woodcock Street in Aston. He was the son of John and Amy Vickers. His father was a tube caster.

Private Vickers originally joined the Royal Warwickshire Regiment in 1902 as a private soldier and had served for six years. On leaving the army he worked for GEC at Witton. He re enlisted when the First World War broke out and rejoined his unit.

Deed: "For most conspicious bravery on 25th September 1915 during operations before Hulluch.

During an attack by his battalion on the German front line trenches Private Vickers on his own initiative and with the utmost bravery went forward in front of his own company under very heavy shell, rifle and machine gun fire and cut the wires which were holding up a great part of the battalion. Although it was broad daylight at the time he carried out this work standing up. His gallant action contributed largely to the success of the assault".

The action in question was part of the Battle of Loos which ended with the British capturing several square miles of territory in northern France.

Subsequent Career: Private Vickers was also promoted to Lance Corporal and awarded the French military medal for his action.

In December 1915 while he was on leave Lance Corporal Vickers visited his old school in Dartmouth Street where he was welcomed by the teachers and pupils. The headmaster made a speech to the school in which he praised up his old boy's performance while the guest of honour expressed his pleasure at seeing his old school again and asked the boys if they would like to become soldiers. All the boys raised their hands. The whole school then sang the national anthem.

Lance Corporal Vickers was later promoted to sergeant. He died in Birmingham on the 27th of July 1944 at the age of 62.

Private Turrall

Full name and unit: Private Thomas George Turrall, the 10th Battalion, the Worcestershire Regiment.

Background: Private Turrall was born in Hay Mills in Birmingham on the 5th of July 1885. His parents later moved to live in Small Heath where his father worked as a labourer for B.S.A.

The young Thomas Turrall attended Dixon Road School. On leaving school he became a painter and decorator. At the outbreak of war he was married with a baby daughter and was living in Yardley.

Thomas Turrall joined up in December 1914 and went to France in September 1915. Shortly after he went abroad his young wife fell ill. He was given leave to go and see her but shortly after his leave expired and he had to return to France she died.

Deed: On the 3rd of July 1916 during the Battle of the Somme "for most conspicious bravery and devotion to duty. During a bombing attack by a small party against the enemy the officer in charge was badly wounded and the party having penetrated the position to a great depth was eventually compelled to retire.

Private Turrall remained with the wounded officer for three hours under continous and very heavy fire from machine guns and bombs and not withstanding that both himself and the officer were at one time completely cut off from our troops he held to his ground with determination and finally carried the officer into our lines after our counter-attacks had made this possible".

The attack in question was a night attack. The officer in question was Turrall's platoon officer Lieutenant Richard Jennings. Lieutenant Jennings was the son of the Vicar of Stonehouse in Gloucestershire and was a former Oxford University boxing champion. He died of his wounds a few hours after he had been brought back but he was able to give a full report of what had happened before he died.

Private Turrall took his baby daughter with him when he went to Buckingham Palace to receive the VC and he was also accompanied by his parents. After the war he returned to his old trade of being a painter and decorator and attended many military reunions.

He died in Selly Oak Hospital on the 21st of February 1964 and was given a full military funeral at the Robin Hood Cemetary in Solihull. He was 78.

Sergeant Gill

Full Name and Unit: Sergeant Albert Gill the 1st Battalion the King's Royal Rifle Corps.

Background: Sergeant Gill was born in 83 Hospital Street in Birmingham (it runs off Summer Lane) on the 8th of September 1879. His father was a corrugated iron worker.

At the outbreak of war Albert Gill was working as a postman in the Hockley area of Birmingham. He was a reservist and was recalled to the forces.

Deed: On the 27th of July 1916 at Delville Wood during the Battle of the Somme "for most conspicious bravery. The enemy made a very strong counter-attack on the right flank of the battalion and rushed the bombing post after killing all the company bombers.

Sergeant Gill at once rallied the remnants of his platoon none of whom were trained bombers and reorganised his defences a most difficult and dangerous task the trench being very shallow and much damaged. Soon afterwards the enemy nearly surrounded his men by creeping up through the thick undergrowth and commenced sniping at about twenty yards range. Although it was almost certain death Sergeant Gill stood boldly up in order to direct the fire of his men. He was killed almost at once but not before he had shown his men where the enemy were and thus enabled them to hold up their advance.

By his supreme devotion to duty and self-sacrifice he saved a very dangerous situation".

Sergeant Gill was 36 when he was killed and left behind a widow. They had had two children but both had died in infancy. Sergeant Gill was buried in Delville Wood Cemetary in France.

Sergeant Knight

Full Name and Unit: Sergeant Alfred Joseph Knight 2nd Eighth Battalion the London Regiment. This unit was better known as the Post Office Rifles.

Background: Sergeant Alfred Joseph Knight was born in Ladywood on the 24th of August 1888. Although he was born a Brummie at the time when he joined the army he was working for the Post Office in Nottingham.

Deed: On the 20th of September 1917 during the third battle of Ypres (ie Passchendaele). "For most conspicious bravery and devotion to duty during the operations against the enemy positions.

Sergeant Knight did extraordinary good work and showed exceptional bravery and initiative when his platoon was attacking an enemy strong point and came under very heavy fire from an enemy machine gun. He rushed through our own barrage, bayonetted the enemy gunner and captured the position single handed.

Later twelve of the enemy with a machine-gun were encountered in a shell-hole. He again rushed forward by himself bayonetted two and shot a third and caused the remainder to scatter.

Subsequently during the attack on a fortified farm when entangled up to his waist in mud and seeing a number of the enemy firing on our troops he immediately opened fire on them without waiting to extricate himself from the mud, killing six of the enemy.

Again noticing the company on his right flank being held up in their attack on another farm Sergeant Knight collected some men and took up a position on the flank of this farm from where he brought a heavy fire to bear on the farm as a result of which the farm was captured.

All the platoon officers of the company had become casualties before the first objective was reached and this gallant NCO took command of all the men of his own platoon and of the platoons without officers. His energy in consolidating and reorganising was untiring.

His several single handed actions showed exceptional bravery and saved a great number of casualties in the company. They were performed under heavy machine gun and rifle fire and without regard to personal risk, and were the direct cause of the objectives being captured".

Subsequent Career: Sergeant Knight was promoted to second-Lieutenant. He died in Birmingham on the 4th of December 1960 at the age of 72.

Sergeant Finch

Full Name and Unit: Sergeant Norman Augustus Finch, Royal Marine Artillery, HMS Vindictive.

Sergeant Finch was born in Nineveh Road in Handsworth on the 26th of December 1890. He was the son of Richard William John Finch who was a postman and Emma Amelia Finch.

Young Norman Finch was educated at Benson Road and Norton Street Council Schools. He joined the navy in 1908 and served on the China station and during the first two years of the war in the North Sea.

Service in the North Sea meant constant danger from submarines and mines and after enduring two years of the strain Sergeant Finch's nerves gave way and he was transferred to shore service. However in 1918 he volunteered to take part in attacks on German occupied Zeebrugge and Ostend.

Deed: On the 22nd to 23rd of April 1918 "For most conspicious gallantry. Sergeant Finch was second in command of the pompoms and Lewis guns in the foretop of "Vindictive" under Lieutenant Charles N. B. Rigby R.M.A. At one period the "Vindictive" was being hit every few seconds, chiefly in the upper works, from which splinters caused many casualties. It was difficult to locate the guns which were doing the most damage but Lieutenant Rigby, Sergeant Finch and the marines in the foretop kept up a continous fire with pompoms and Lewis guns changing rapidly from one target to another and thus keeping the enemy's fire down to some considerable extent.

Unfortunately two heavy shells made direct hits on the foretop which was completely exposed to enemy concentration of fire. All in

17

the top were killed or disabled except Sergeant Finch who was however severely wounded; nevertheless he showed consummate bravery remaining in his battered and exposed position. He once more got a Lewis gun into action and kept up a continous fire harassing the enemy on the mole until the foretop received another direct hit the remainder of the armanent being then completely put out of action. Before the top was destroyed Sergeant Finch had done invaluable work and by his bravery undoubtedly saved many lives.

This very gallant sergeant of the Royal Marine Artillery was selected by the 4th Battalion of Royal Marines who were mostly Royal Marine Light Infantry to receive the Victoria Cross under Rule 13 of the Royal Warrant dated 29th January 1856".

Subsequent Career: Sergeant Finch was wounded and was treated in Deal hospital where he received a visit from Admiral Keyes who had commanded the attacks against Ostend and Zeebrugge and who was a very well known naval hero.

Sergeant Finch was promoted to be a Lieutenant and Quartermaster and served in the navy until 1945. In 1961 he became a Sergeant-Major in the Queen's Bodyguard of the Yeoman of the Guard. After his retirement he lived in Portsmouth where a Finch Road was named after him. He died in Portsmouth on the 15th of March 1966 at the age of 75.

Lance-Corporal Onions

Full Name and Unit: Lance-Corporal George Onions, the 1st Battalion, the Devonshire Regiment.

Background: George Onions was the son of Zachariah Webb Onions who was a Bilston iron master and his wife Amy Susan Onions and he was born in Wellington Street in Bilston on the 2nd March 1883 (his connection to our city came later). His family later moved to South Wales in connection with the iron trade and he was educated at West Monmouthshire Grammar School in Pontypool. After leaving school he set up in business as an iron and steel merchant.

On the 5th of September 1914 he joined the army as a private soldier. He first joined the 3rd King's Own Hussars but in 1917 he was transferred to the Devonshire Regiment by which time it was policy to stop putting men from one area into one unit. By this time he had been promoted to be a Lance-Corporal.

Deed: "For most conspicious bravery and initiative south of Achiet-le Petitiet on 22nd August 1918 when having been sent out with one man to get in touch with the battalion on the right flank he observed the enemy advancing in large numbers to counter-attack the positions gained on the previous day.

Realising his opportunity he boldly placed himself with his comrade on the flank of the advancing enemy and opened rapid fire when the target was most favourable. When the enemy were about 100 yards from him, the line wavered and some hands were seen to be thrown up. Lance Corporal Onions then rushed forward and with the assistance of his comrade, took about 200 of the enemy prisoners and marched them back to his company commander.

By his magnificent courage and presence of mind he averted what might have been a very dangerous situation".

Subsequent Career: Lance-Corporal Onions was promoted to be an officer and was demobilised in February 1919. He became an iron and steel merchant again and moved to live in Birmingham. He rejoined the army in 1939 and by 1941 he was a major at which point he resigned his commission because of ill health and became a Home Guard Officer. He died in a Birmingham hospital on the 2nd April 1944. He was 61.

Sergeant Colley

Full Name and Unit: Private (Acting-Sergeant) Harold John Colley, the 10th Battalion, The Lancashire Fusiliers.

Background: Harold Colley was born in Smethwick on the 26th of May 1894

Deed: On the 25th of August 1918 at Martinpuich in France "For most conspicious bravery and initiative when in command of a platoon in support of forward platoons which had been ordered to hold on at all costs.

19

When the enemy counter-attacked in force he rushed forward on his own initiative to help the forward line rallying and controlling the men holding it. The enemy by this time were advancing quickly and had already obtained a footing in the trench. Sergeant Colley then formed a defensive flank and held it. Out of the two platoons only three men remained unwounded and he himself was dangerously wounded.

It was entirely due to Sergeant Colley's action that the enemy were prevented from breaking through and were eventually driven off. His courage and tenacity saved a very critical situation".

Sergeant Colley died later that day of his wounds at the age of 24. He was buried at Maily Wood Cemetary in France.

Lance Corporal Wilcox

Full Name and Unit: Lance Corporal Alfred Wilcox the 2nd 4th Battalion the Oxfordshire and Buckinghamshire Light Infantry.

Background: Alfred Wilcox was born in a back to back house behind Wilton Street in Aston on the 16th of December 1884. He was the son of William and Sarah Ann Wilcox. His father worked in the jewellery quarter.

Alfred Wilcox was educated at the Burlington Street School in Aston. On leaving school he worked as a diamond mounter for E. Durban and Co. in Frederick Street. He later moved to London and joined up in March 1915. His wife and two children then moved back to Birmingham and lived in Small Heath presumably to be closer to their relatives.

Deed: On the 12th September 1918 near Laventie in France "For most conspicious bravery and initiative in attack when his company was held up by heavy and persistent machine gun fire at close range.

On his own initiative with four men he rushed ahead to the nearest enemy gun, bombed it killed the gunner and put the gun out of action. Being then attacked by an enemy bombing party Corporal Wilcox picked up enemy bombs and led his party against the next gun finally capturing and destroying it.

Although left with only one man he continued bombing and captured a third gun. He again bombed up the trench, captured a fourth gun and then rejoined his platoon.

Corporal Wilcox displayed in this series of successful individual enterprises exceptional valour judgement and initiative".

Subsequent Career: Lance-Corporal Wilcox died in Birmingham on the 30th of March 1951. He was 66.

Lance-Corporal Amey

Full Name and Unit: Lance Corporal William Amey the first eighth battalion, the Royal Warwickshire Regiment (he was a territorial).

Background: William Amey was born in Mount Street in Duddeston on the 5th of March 1881. He was the son of Charles Amey who was a railway carriage fitter and Elizabeth Amey.

Deed: "For most conspicious bravery on 4th November 1918 during the attack on Landrecies when owing to fog many hostile machine gun nests were missed by the leading troops.

On his own initiative he led his section against a machine gun nest under heavy fire, drove the garrison into a neighbouring farm and finally captured about 50 prisoners and several machine guns.

Later single handed and under heavy fire he attacked a machine gun post in a farmhouse, killed two of the garrison, and drove the remainder into a cellar until assistance arrived.

Subsequently, single handed he rushed a strongly held post capturing twenty prisoners. He displayed throughout the day the highest degree of valour and determination".

Subsequent Career: Lance-Corporal Amey was promoted to Corporal. He died in Leamington Spa on the 28th of May 1940 at the age of 59.

Lieutenant-Colonel Marshall

Full Name and Unit: Acting Lieutenant-Colonel John Neville Marshall, the Irish Guards attached to the 16th Battalion, The Lancashire Fusiliers.

Background: John Marshall was born in Stratford on the 12th of June 1887. He was educated at Wellesbourne House School in Acocks Green and at Camp Hill Grammar School. His first job was as a clerk at the Birmingham and Midland Institute and he then got a job as a clerk at the Birmingham University Medical Faculty. Having put some money aside he left this job in 1904 to study veterinary science and later practised as a vet at Harlow in Essex. At the outbreak of the war he was employed by the War Office Remounts Department and his job was purchasing horses from the Argentine. This was a job which carried officer rank.

During the course of the war John Marshall was transferred to the Irish Guards. He was wounded ten times, won the Military Cross and Bar and gained rapid promotion and eventually became an Acting Lieutenant-Colonel with the Lancashire Fusiliers.

Deed: "For most conspicious bravery, determination and leadership in the attack on the Sambre-Oise Canal near Catillon on the 4th November 1918 when a partly constructed bridge came under concentrated fire and was broken before the advanced troops of the battalion could cross.

Lieutenant-Colonel Marshall at once went forward and organised parties to repair the bridge.

The first party were soon killed or wounded but by personal example he inspired his command and volunteers were instantly forthcoming.

Under intense fire and with complete disregard of his own safety he stood on the bank encouraging his men and assisting in the work and when the bridge was repaired attempted to rush across at the head of his battalion and was killed while so doing.

The passage of the canal was of vital importance and the gallantry displayed by all ranks was largely due to the inspiring example set by Lieutenant-Colonel Marshall".

The gallant Lieutenant-Colonel Marshall was buried at Ors Communal Cemetary in France. Apart from his British medals he was also a holder of the French Croix de Guerre and the Belgian Chevalier of the Order of Leopold.

Captain Waters

Full name and unit: Captain (Acting Major) Arnold Horace Santo Waters 218th Field Company, Royal Engineers.

Background: Captain Waters was born in Plymouth on the 23rd of September 1886. He was the son of the Reverend Richard Waters of the United Reformed Church and was educated at Hoe Grammar School in Plymouth. He became an engineer and started working for the Birmlngham consulting engineering firm of Willcox and Raikes.

Deed: "For most conspicious bravery and devotion to duty on the 4th November 1918 near Ors when bridging with his Field Company the Oise-Sambre Canal. From the outset the task was under artillery and machine gun fire at close range the bridge being damaged and the building party suffering severe casualties. Major Waters hearing that all his officers had been killed or wounded at once went forward and personally supervised the completion of the bridge working on cork floats while under fire at point blank range. So intense was the fire that it seemed impossible that he could escape being killed. The success of the operation was due entirely to his valour and example".

Subsequent Career: Captain Waters continued his career as an engineer after the war and lived in Sutton Coldfield. In 1933 he was president of the Institute of Structural Engineers and during the Second World War he was Divisional Food Officer for the West Midlands. From 1946 to 1959 he was chairman of the South Staffordshire Waterworks Company. He was a Sutton Coldfield JP and a Deputy Lieutenant of Warwickshire. In 1954 he was awarded a knighthood for his civilian services. He died on the 22nd of January 1981 at the age of 94 and was the last surviving First World War VC with Birmingham connections.

One of Britain's leading war poets Wilfred Owen was killed the same day during an attempt to cross the Oise-Sambre canal at another point.

EGION." GERMANY'S WAR GUILT. OFFICER HEROES. THE CO

ed & Freed | Letters from Kaiser to Czar and King George.

Birmingham Associations of Latest V.C.s.

Improveme Early

TRIBUTE.

(Continued from Page One.)

of Europe in order, if possible, to avoid war, and his conversations with the German Ambassador in London, in which he stated: "If we thought British interests required us to intervene we must intervene at once."

salvation of a overnment and ver forget it.".

onceau acknows Douglas Haig, by the British lation liberated 1 October to 25

ng a copy of the on attached to hat the British r four days the r 700,000 souls their country. ed enough, and ı over five, mil buted by the able lives were ore and nurses, in their efforts pidemic of in press all that st unceasingly g, endured in sistance to our

Kaiser to the Czar.

The telegram of 30 July, 1914 from Sir Edward Grey to the British Ambassador at Berlin declining to refrain from hostilities on terms, which Sir Edward styled "a disgrace from which the good name of Britain would never recover," is reproduced, and Professor Oman's remark on it is: "It was very difficult to convince the German Foreign Office that the policy of a British Liberal Government would not, in the end, be determined by the wish to keep out of the trouble at all costs."

On the same date the Kaiser wired to the Czar:

Austria-Hungary was mobilised only against Serbia—and only part of her army. If Russia mobilises against Austria-Hungary, the part of a mediator which I have accepted on your express desire is threatened if not made impossible. You now have to bear the responsibility for war or peace.

The Czar, according to the narrative, endeavoured to cancel general mobilisation, and it was intimated to him that it had been done.

ts Fed. on shows that they advanced, ts for the pro laces were the osition to take eleaged people before the first d, and during the difficulties n several occa ish troops to , the British k of carrying , distributing lity of 5,904,000

From evidence subsequently given by the Russian General Sukhominoff, he is reported to have said: "Next morning I lied to the Czar and explained to him that mobilisation was in full swing and that in the districts of the south-west. On this day I nearly lost my reason. I knew that mobilisation was in full swing and that it was impossible to stop it. Fortunately on the same day the Czar was convinced afresh and I was thanked for the good execution of the mobilisation. Otherwise I should long ago have been in gaol."

eretofore," the his way from French people and had syste mes of sub

A Hellweg Telegram.

Professor Oman then states:—On the 1st August the subjoined telegram, ostensibly from the German Chancellor to Herr von Tschirsky, the German Ambassador at Vienna, was published in the "Westminster Gazette," and there alone:—

AN OLD CAMP HILL BOY.

The two latest awards of the V.C. to officers who were directly associated with Birmingham.

Captain (Acting Major) Arnold Horace Santo Waters, V.C., D.S.O., M.C., 218th Field Co., R.E., was for five years prior to receiving his commission a member of the engineering staff of Messrs. Wilcox and Raikes, of Birmingham. A native of Lostwithiel (Cornwall), and the son of a Wesleyan minister, Capt. Waters was in the early stages of the war engaged upon important work on Salisbury Plain, where he had been in charge of an engineering staff engaged in supervising the construction of new water supplies for the troops.

CAPT. WATERS.

The V.C. was awarded him for most conspicuous bravery and devotion to duty on 4 November, 1918, near Ors, when bridging with his Field Company the Oise-Sambre Canal.

The late Lieut. (Acting Lieut.-Col.) John Neville Marshall, M.C., late Irish Guards (S.R.), attached 16th Batt. Lancashire Fusiliers, was the son of the late Mr. J. Neville Marshall and Mrs. Marshall, Eastbourne House, Warwick-road, Acock's Green. Born in that village about 30 years ago, Lieut. Marshall was educated at Wellesbourne House School and Camp Hill Grammar School. His first business position was clerk in the Birmingham and Midland Institute.

After a short stay there he accepted a position on the clerical staff of the Birmingham University Medical Faculty, which he occupied until 1904. Subsequently he took up veterinary work, and for several years had a successful practice at Harlow, Essex. At the outbreak of war he was serving with one of the Scottish Regiments, being engaged by the War Office Remount Department purchasing horses in the Argentine.

Later he was transferred to the Irish Guards, and while on active service gained rapid promotion. In the early part of last autumn his gallant conduct won for him the M.C. Lieut. Marshall must have had many narrow escapes, for prior to performing the heroic deed which cost him his life on the Sambre-Oise Canal on 4 November last, he had been wounded on ten different occasions.

BABY-DROWNED.

PATHETIC STORY AT BROMSGROVE INQUEST.

A pathetic story was unfolded at an inquest at Bromsgrove last night relative to the tragic drowning of Maurice Pinfield, the 18 months old child of William and Florence Pinfield, who lived at Green Vale Farm, Catshill, near Bromsgrove. Mrs. Mary Field, the grandmother of the deceased baby, is at present in Bromsgrove

While no in supply can be Birmingham du H. Humphries, t made the welco substantial en expected early made strenuous of these supplie canals frozen up some of the can certain amount A gradual impr plies is, however Asked if he ha at the local f replied that whi single instance had been report schools were con made a special supplies for the An official at t stated that whil time during the plies, they had close one so In one or two i closed owing to in the heating would see the w swing again.

£25

BUTLER'S H

A sidelight on derived from t mingham Polic application to Granted to Mr City-road, Edgl husband, who is Knutsford.

Before we w the magistrates, money in the ba the cash in his he had got £25 when he was w The Bench de

COUNCI

POLLING TA THREE

Polling takes the Birminghan tatives for the Small Heath, a The candidate Small Heath: and Mr. J. H 159, Waverley-r Saltley: Mr. 14, Bowyer-road Adderley-road, ham branch of of Discharged and Soldiers. Duddeston a Sawyer (Labou Charles Keatl Erdington loca Workers' Natio Speaking in j F. Sawyer urge concern of the voted to the o

Able Seaman Savage

Full Name and Unit: Able Seaman William Alfred Savage,
Motor Gun Boat 314.

Background: Able Seaman Savage was born in Smethwick on the
30th of October 1912. During the Second World War he took part in
the raid on German facilities in the French port of St Nazaire on the
27th of March 1942.

Deed: "For great gallantry, skill and devotion to duty as gunlayer of
the pom-pom in a motor gun boat in the St Nazaire raid. Completely
exposed and under heavy fire he engaged positions ashore with cool
and steady accuracy. On the way out of the harbour he kept up the
same vigorous and accurate fire against the attacking ships until he
was killed at his gun.

This Victoria Cross is awarded in recognition not only of the
gallantry and devotion to duty of Able Seaman Savage but also of
the valour shown by many others unnamed in motor launches,
motor gun boats and motor torpedo boats who gallantly carried out
their duty in entirely exposed positions against enemy fire at very
close range".

The body of Able Seaman Savage was brought back to England and
buried in Falmouth cemetary.

More than a hundred men won various different medals for their
part in this raid. One such was nineteen year old Seaman A B. Smith
of Harborne who was manning the same gun as Able Seaman
Savage and who won the Distinguished Service Medal. He was
interviewed by the "Birmingham Evening Mail" and said that "We
circled the harbour for an hour firing all the while at gun posts.
Everything the Germans had they flung at us and we had a warm
time!".

Lieutenant Colonel Foote

Full Name and Unit:
Acting Lieutenant Colonel Henry Bowreman Foote, The Royal Tank
Regiment.
Background: Henry Foote was born at Ishapur in Bengal in India on

the 5th of December 1904 (his connection with Birmingham will be explained below) where his father Lieutenant Colonel Henry Bruce Foote was the superintendant of a rifle factory. His mother died when he was very young and his father remarried.

The young Henry Foote junior was educated at St Cyprian's School, Eastbourne and Bedford Public School where he was a keen athlete and head of his house. He joined the Army and went to Sandhurst at the age of 19. On becoming an officer he joined the Royal Tank Corps and became a second lieutenant in 1925, a first lieutenant in 1927 and a Captain in 1936.

Captain Foote studied at the Staff College in 1939 and later in 1939 he became a GSO3 (General Staff Officer 3) at the War Office. He became a GSO2 at the War Office in 1940 and later in 1940 a GSO2 at the Staff College. In 1941 he became the GSO1 for the 10th Armoured Division and in 1942 he became the officer in command of the 7th Royal Tank Regiment. By this time he was a substantive major and an acting Lieutenant Colonel.

Deed: "For outstanding gallantry during the period 27th May to 15th June 1942.

On the 6th June, Lieutenant Colonel Foote led his battalion which had been subjected to very heavy artillery fire in pursuit of a superior force of enemy while changing to another tank after his own had been knocked out Lieutenant Colonel Foote was wounded in the neck. In spite of this he continued to lead his battalion from an exposed position on the outside of a tank.

The enemy who were holding a strongly entrenched position with anti-tank guns attacked his flank. As a further tank had been disabled he continued on foot under intense fire encouraging his men by his splendid example. By dusk Lieutenant Colonel Foote by his brilliant leadership had defeated the enemy's attempt to encircle two of our divisions.

By 13th June when ordered to delay the enemy tanks so that the guards brigade could be withdrawn from the Knightsbridge escarpment and when the first wave of our tanks had been destroyed, Lieutenant-Colonel Foote reorganised the remaining tanks going on foot from one tank to another to encourage the crews under intense artillery and tank fire.

As it was of vital importance that his battalion should not give ground Lieutenant Colonel Foote placed his tank which he had then entered in front of the others so that he could be plainly visible in the turret as an encouragement to the other crews inspite of the tank being badly damaged by shell fire and all its guns rendered useless. By his magnificent example the corridor was kept open and the brigade was able to march through.

Lieutenant Colonel Foote was always at the crucial point at the right moment and over a period of several days gave an example of outstanding courage and leadership which it would have been difficult to surpass. His name was a byword for bravery and leadership throughout the brigade".

Subsequent Career: Later in June 1942 Tobruk fell and Lieutenant Colonel Foote and four other soldiers attempted to escape. They got through the German lines but Lieutenant Colonel Foote broke his leg trying to climb down into a wadi and later the same day they were captured by the Germans.

Lieutenant Colonel Foote was handed over to the Italians but in September 1943 the Italians capitulated and he was released. He tried to make his way south over the mountains to the British lines but the snow made this impossible and he retraced his steps and crossed into Switzerland in November 1943. He was interned in Switzerland but was released in October 1944, along with 5,000 other internees.

On his release Lieutenant Colonel Foote returned home to a family home that he had never seen before. By this time his step mother and half sister were living at 187, Ladywood Road in Edgbaston where his half sister Miss S.M Foote was a modern languages teacher at Edgbaston High School. They had moved to Birmingham from Surrey. Another of his sisters Miss J. Foote BSc was a science lecturer at Achimota College in what was then called the Gold Coast and is now called Ghana.

Once he had recovered Lieutenant Colonel Foote was appointed GSO1 at Air Force Headquarters in Italy and in 1945 he became second in command of the 9th Armoured Brigade. Later appointments included being officer in command of the automotive wing of the Fighting Vehicles Proving Establishment at the Ministry of Supply from 1948 to 1949, commander of the seventh armoured brigade from 1949 to 1950, commander of the eleventh armoured division from 1950 to 1953, director-general of fighting vehicles at the Ministry of Supply from 1953 to 1955 and director of the Royal Armoured Corps at the War Office from 1955 to 1958. By this time he was a major-general.

Major-General Foote is still alive and lives in Sussex.

Lance Corporal Kenneally

Full Name and Unit: Lance Corporal John Patrick Kenneally, Irish Guards.

Background: John Kenneally was born in Birmingham on the 15th of March 1921 and joined the Irish Guards at the age of 17.

Deed: "The Bou feature dominates all ground east and west between Medjez El Bab and Tebourba. It was essential to the final assault on Tunis that this feature should be captured and held.

A Guards Brigade assaulted and captured a portion of the Bou on the 27th April 1943. The Irish Guards held on to points 212 and 214 at the western end of the feature which points the Germans frequently counter-attacked. While a further attack to capture the complete feature was being prepared it was essential for the Irish Guards to hold on. They did so.

On the 28th April 1943 the positions held by one company of the Irish Guards on the ridge between points 212 and 214 were about to be subjected to an attack by the enemy. Approximately one company of the enemy were seen forming up preparatory to attack and Lance-Corporal Kenneally decided that this was the right moment to attack them himself. Single handed he charged down the bare forward slope straight at the main enemy body firing his bren gun from the hip as he did so. This outstanding act of gallantry and the dash with which it was executed completely unbalanced the enemy company which broke up in disorder. Lance-Corporal Kenneally then returned to the crest further to harass their retreat.

Lance Corporal Kenneally repeated this remarkable exploit on the morning of the 30th April 1943 when accompanied by a Sergeant of the Reconnaissance Corps he again charged the enemy forming up for an assault. This time he so harassed the enemy inflicting many casualties that this projected assault was frustrated: the enemy's strength was again about one company. It was only when he was noticed hopping from one fire position to another further to the left in order to support another company carrying his gun in one hand and supporting himself on a guardsman with the other was it discovered he had been wounded. He refused to give up his bren gun claiming that he was the only one who understood that gun and continued to fight all through that day with great courage, devotion to duty and disregard for his own safety.

The magnificent gallantry of this NCO on these two occasions under heavy fire his unfailing vigilance and remarkable accuracy were responsible for saving many valuable lives during the days and nights in the forward positions. His actions also played a considerable part in holding these positions and this influenced the whole course of the battle. His rapid appreciation of the situation, his initiative and his extraordinary gallantry in attacking single-handed a massed body of the enemy and breaking up an attack on two occasions was an achievement that can seldom have been equalled. His courage in fighting all day when wounded was an inspiration to all ranks". © Crown copyright 1993/MOD reproduced with the permission of the Controller of H.M.S.O.

Subsequent Career: Lance Corporal Kenneally was later promoted to Company Quarter Master Sergeant. No further information is available as to his later career.

The George Cross

The George Cross was established by King George VI on the 24th September 1940. It can be awarded to people who show supreme courage in circumstances which do not qualify them for the VC which can only be awarded for courage displayed in the face of the enemy.

When the George Cross was founded a previous award called the Empire Gallantry Medal was abolished and all holders were required to return their medals and exchange them for the new award. In 1971 two more medals the Edward Medal and the Albert Medal were abolished and their holders placed on the roll of the George Cross. Holders of these medals were allowed either to exchange their medal for a George Cross or keep it and at the same time be entitled to say that they held the George Cross. The Albert Medal had been granted for saving life at sea or on land and the Edward Medal was granted for bravery during industrial accidents.

Up to 1985 a total of 396 men and women had won the George Cross or had won other medals and been placed on the GC roll. Of the 152 people who won the George Cross directly 103 were service personnel and 49 were civilians. In addition to the George Cross the George Medal can also be awarded for acts of courage by service personnel or civilians and its award is more frequent than is that of the George Cross.

The George Cross is made of silver and is inscribed with the words "For Gallantry". It is worn suspended from a one and a half inches wide dark blue ribbon. It takes precedence over all medals except for the Victoria Cross.

Like the VC, GC winners have come from a wide range of backgrounds. Like the winners of the VC they are all united by courage.

Private Miller

Full Name and Unit: Private Thomas Frank Miller, the 2nd Battalion, the Dorset Regiment.

Background: Private Miller was born in Portland in Dorset on the 7th October 1887 (he moved to Birmingham later). He was a regular soldier and served in the army both during the First World War and later.

After the Indian Mutiny was defeated in 1857 Indian nationalism developed as a movement of peaceful protest and non violent direct action. However there were isolated armed uprisings. One such uprising occurred in Malabar in 1921. Crushing it required the services of four battalions of infantry including the 2nd Dorsetshires, a battery of artillery, a section of armoured cars and other units. Forty three government troops were killed and a hundred and twenty six wounded and the rebels also suffered heavy casualties.

Deed: On the 24th September 1921 the advanced guard of a column of British troops was ambushed. Private Miller charged the ambushing force and shot and killed several snipers.

Private Miller was awarded the Empire Gallantry Medal. In 1940 this was converted into a George Cross.

Subsequent Career: Thomas Miller died in Birmingham on the 13th of November 1974 at the age of 87.

Flying Officer Graveley

Full Name and Unit: Flying Officer Reginald Cubitt Graveley, 88 Squadron, Royal Air Force.

Background: Reginald Graveley was born in Leyton in London in March 1914. He joined the air force in 1935 and was commissioned in 1936.

Deed: "This officer displayed great gallantry and a total disregard of his own safety when the aircraft of which he was the pilot was shot down by an enemy fighter in September 1939 and crashed in flames. Though badly burned he pulled his wounded air observer from the wreckage to a place of safety and then returned to rescue the air gunner. He found the airman dead however and was unable to lift him from the cockpit".

Subsequent Career: Reginald Graveley was awarded the Empire Gallantry Medal by King George VI. He was later given the George Cross and asked to return the Empire Gallantry Medal but he was so upset by this decision that he was allowed to keep his former medal as well though he was told that he should wear the George Cross rather than the Empire Gallantry Medal.

Reginald Graveley became involved in aerial photography and later became Senior Photographic Officer to the Photographic Reconnaissance Unit. This unit took pictures of bombed German cities to show what damage had been done.

After a year of photographic work Reginald Graveley visited the USA to be a liaison officer to the then United States Army Air Corps. After this job he resigned from the air force to become a Test Pilot for the Gloster Aircraft Company. He later joined the Brockhouse Organisation which was a group of companies which were heavily involved in war contracts and whose headquarters were at West Bromwich. It was in this connection that he moved to Birmingham.

Reginald Graveley died on the 16th September 1961 at the age of 47.

Lieutenant Reynolds

Full Name and Unit: Lieutenant Edward Womersley Reynolds, 101 and 102 Bomb Disposal Sections, Corps of Royal Engineers.

Background: Edward Reynolds was born in Birmingham on the 27th of June 1917. He was the grandson of Alderman A. J. Reynolds who was Lord Mayor of Birmingham in 1906 and the son of Mr and Mrs J.H. Reynolds. Mr Reynolds was Honorary Secretary of the Birmingham and Midland Institute and Honorary Treasurer of the Royal Astronomical Society.

The young Edward Reynolds was educated at West House School in Edgbaston and the famous Repton public school in Derbyshire. On leaving work he got a job with the family firm Reynolds and Co. He joined the Territorial Army Royal Engineers and during the war he was a bomb disposal officer.

Deed: "On 17th August 1940 a 250 kilo bomb fell in a garden amongst some council houses; it did not explode and Lieutenant Reynolds was sent to investigate. On digging down 17 feet he found that it had a new type of fuse about which no instructions had at that time been received. Finding that traffic was suspended on the road and that the inhabitants had had to be cleared out of their houses he removed the fuse and found that it had a clockwork delayed action. The risk that he took was great and the merit of his action was the greater for lack of exact knowledge of the type of fuse he was dealing with.

On 3rd September 1940 - A large bomb fell in a street just before midnight on September 1st 1940; it wrecked the front of some business premises and was supposed to have exploded. About 16.30 hours on the 3rd September a 250 kilo unexploded bomb was found in the debris. Lieutenant Reynolds was at once summoned found that it had a clockwork fuse which was still ticking and according to orders applied to Regional HQ for instructions suggesting that the sooner it was dealt with the better and stating that he was willing to do so forthwith. In view of the damage to property that would have been caused by the explosion of such a large bomb in such a congested area and especially of the possible effect on the public morale permission was given and Lieutenant Reynolds immediately extracted the fuse and rendered the bomb inoperative. The risk in doing this was very considerable".

Lieutenant Reynolds was originally awarded the Empire Gallantry Medal but this was converted into a GC.

Subsequent Career: Lieutenant Reynolds finished his military career as Major Reynolds. He died on the 16th December 1955. He was 38

Acting Squadron Leader Moxey

Full Name and Unit: Acting Squadron Leader Eric Laurence Moxey, the Royal Air Force Volunteer Reserve.

Background: Eric Moxey was born at Sao Paulo in Brazil on the 14th of April 1894 and during World War One he served with the Yorkshire & Lancashire Regiment and the Royal Flying Corps.

Deed: "On the 27th August 1940 it was reported that two unexploded bombs were embedded in an aerodrome. Squadron Leader Moxey, a technical intelligence officer employed at the Air Ministry, immediately volunteered to proceed to the site and remove them though from the nature of his duties he was very fully aware of the risk entailed in such an operation. One of the bombs exploded causing his death. On many occasions Squadron Leader Moxey has exhibited similar complete disregard for his personal safety".

The airfield in question was the famous Biggin Hill in Kent which was not named by the London Gazette because it was publishcd in war time and copies invariably found their way into Germany where expert newspaper analysts studied it to see what information they could obtain.

Acting Squadron Leader Moxey was buried at the churchyard of the church of St Peter and Paul at Cudham in Kent. He was 46 when he died. Although he was not a Birmingham man himself he had strong connections with Birmingham according to "The Register of the George Cross" although this does not go into any details about these connections.

Section Commander Inwood

Full Name and Unit: Section Commander George Walter Inwood, 30th Warwickshire Battalion, The Home Guard.

Background: George Inwood was born in Birmingharn on the 14th of September 1906.

Deed: During the night of the 15th to the 16th of October 1940 there was a heavy German air raid on Birmingham. George Inwood took his section to help rescue trapped survivors and discovered that several people were trapped in a cellar under a house which had been bombed. Gas had leaked into the cellar from a bomb damaged gas main and its occupants were unconscious.

George Inwood went into the cellar twice and rescued two men. Despite being under the influence of the gas himself he insisted on going down a third time. He then collapsed and died.

George Inwood was the only member of Birmingham's Home Guard to win the George Cross while carrying out his duties. He was buried in Yardley Cemetary.

Station Officer Mosedale

Full Name and Unit: Station Officer William Mosedale, Birmingham Fire Brigade.

Background: William Mosedale was born on the 28th of March 1894. He joined the Birmingham Fire Brigade in 1914 and became a specialist rescue and breathing apparatus expert.

Deed: On the night of the 12th December 1940 "An Auxiliary Fire Station was completely demolished by a very large high explosive

SUPPLEMENT

TO

The London Gazette

Of TUESDAY, the 25th of MARCH 1941

Published by Authority

Registered as a newspaper

FRIDAY, 28 MARCH, 1941

CENTRAL CHANCERY OF THE ORDERS
OF KNIGHTHOOD.

St. James's Palace, S.W.1.
28th March, 1941.

The KING has been graciously pleased to
award the GEORGE CROSS to:—

a Mosedale, Station Officer and Rescue
Officer, Birmingham Fire Brigade.

An Auxiliary Fire Station was completely
demolished by a very large high explosive
bomb. A number of Auxiliary Firemen
were trapped in the station and civilians
were buried in an adjoining house which had
also been demolished.

Station Officer Mosedale immediately began
tunnelling and propping operations. Hundreds of tons of debris covered the site and
Mosedale fully realised that at any moment
he might be buried by a further collapse.

When the first tunnel was completed and
the Control Room reached, he found that
there were still men whom he could not extricate. He carried out another tunnelling
operation from a different direction and again
entered the Control Room. Five men were
found, one dead, the others injured.

The Station Officer crawled through and
administered oxygen to the injured men and
they were then taken out through the tunnel.

The entrance to the cellar of the private
house was full of debris. Station Officer
Mosedale directed operations for removing
this, only to find that the cellar itself had
collapsed. He nevertheless persevered and,
after a time, reached seven people who were
trapped. Three had been killed outright
when the roof collapsed. He gave oxygen to
the remaining four and succeeded in extricating them.

To reach other victims it was again necessary to tunnel, and Mosedale immediately
commenced this work. The dangers to be
faced were similar to those which he had
found in reaching the Control Room. He
nevertheless completed the tunnel and entered
the cellar under the Fire Station. Four men
who were alive were given oxygen and,
despite their injuries, were safely removed.

Tunnelling through such difficult material
had necessarily been extremely hazardous,
and the cellar collapsed completely, shortly
after the removal of the last victim.

These operations, which lasted more than
twelve hours, were carried out under a most
intense bombardment. Twelve lives were
saved by Station Officer Mosedale who
showed outstanding gallantry and resource.
In effecting the rescues he repeatedly risked
his own life.

bomb. A number of Auxiliary Firemen were trapped in the station and civilians were buried in an adjoining house which had also been demolished.

Station Officer Mosedale immediately began tunnelling and propping operations. Hundreds of tons of debris covered the site and Mosedale fully realised that at any moment he might be buried by a further collapse.

When the first tunnel was completed and the control room reached he found that there were still men whom he could not extricate. He carried out another tunnelling operation from a different direction and again entered the control room. Five men were found one dead, the others injured.

The Station Officer crawled through and administered oxygen to the injured men and they were then taken out through the tunnel. The entrance to the cellar of the private house was full of debris. Station Officer Mosedale directed operations for removing this only to find that the cellar itself had collapsed. He nevertheless persevered and after a time reached seven people who were trapped. Three had been killed outright when the roof collapsed. He gave oxygen to the remaining four and succeeded in extricating them.

To reach other victims it was again necessary to tunnel and Mosedale immediately commenced this work. The dangers to be faced were similar to those which he had found in reaching the Control Room. He nevertheless completed the tunnel and entered the cellar under the Fire Station. Four men who were alive were given oxygen and despite their injuries were safely removed.

Tunnelling through such difficult material had necessarily been extremely hazardous and the cellar collapsed completely shortly after the removal of the last victim.

These operations which lasted more than twelve hours were carried out under a most intense bombardment. Twelve lives were saved by Station Officer Mosedale who showed outstanding gallantry and resource. In effecting the rescues he repeatedly risked his own life".

Subsequent Career: Station Officer Mosedale heard that he was to be given the George Cross on his forty seventh birthday on the 28th of May 1941. He eventually retired and moved to Somerset and he died at Nailsea on the 27th of May 1971. He was just one day off from his seventy seventh birthday. He was interred at Arno's Vale Crematorium.

William Waterson

Full Name and job: William Waterson, Foreman, the General Electric Company, Birmingham.

Background: William Waterson was born in Birmingham in 1904.

Deed: "At 4-30. AM on Saturday the 18th August 1945 two workmen employed in the carbon black plant at the works of the General Electric Co. Ltd. Birmingham were employed in collecting newly manufactured lamp black from a brick chamber. The men were unprotected and had to withstand a high temperature as well as an unpleasant atmosphere due to particles of oily lamp black, while carbon monoxide was present from burning soot. After a short time Webb, one of the workmen, collapsed and his companion Albert Edward Stranks being unable to move him sought assistance. Breathing apparatus was stored at the works fire station some distance away; when Stranks called for help the fire alarm was properly sounded. To await the arrival of breathing apparatus would inevitably have resulted in some delay and as the event conclusively proved there was no time to lose.

William Waterson who was the first to arrive on the scene after the alarm was given joined Stranks and in order to avoid any delay in going to Webb's assistance without hesitation though fully realising the risk entered the chamber and attempted to pull the man out. Webb was covered in sweat and carbon black and rescue work was difficult as it was not possible to get a proper grip on him. They were unsuccessful at first and on coming out Stranks collapsed; but Waterson continued to make attempts, entering four times in all. On his last entry he was accompanied by John Thomas Hewitt a member of the Works Fire Brigade who had then arrived with a rope but not with the breathing apparatus; together they succeeded in bringing Webb out who unfortunately was found to be dead.

The hazards were serious owing to the presence of the carbon monoxide gas, intense heat, complete darkness except for the light from a portable acetylene lamp (the carbon covered surroundings absorb all light and give no reflection), the deposit of the carbon black and the confined space, conditions to which Waterson and Hewitt were unaccustomed.

Both Waterson and Stranks suffered badly from gassing and were removed to hospital and Hewitt suffered to a lesser extent".

William Waterson was awarded the Edward Medal and was entered on the roll of the George Cross in 1971.

Subsequent Career: William Waterson died in Birmingham on the 24th of March 1973 at the age of 68.

Charles Wilcox

Name and job: Charles Wilcox, employed as a painter by Birmingham Corporation.

Background: Charles Wilcox was born on the 11th May 1919 and served in the armed forces during World War Two.

Deed: On Tuesday 23rd August 1949 Mr Charles Wilcox (aged 30) a painter employed by Birmingham Corporation was engaged with other men in painting a Council House building in the centre of the city.

One of the other painters Alfred Leslie Burrows (aged 21) mounted a ladder to begin painting an exterior window on the third floor of the building and at the top of the ladder about forty five feet above the street climbed onto an arched sill about eighteen inches width which was sited below the window. He then found that the window was bricked up from the inside and that there was nothing for him to hold to enable him to retain his balance. He turned round to return to the ladder but could not see it, became frightened and crouched down trying to retain his balance on the ledge.

The foreman painter saw Burrows' predicament and sent another painter to his assistance but this man returned to the ground after supporting Burrows for a few minutes. Charles Wilcox then climbed the ladder to assist Burrows and by kneeling on a flat piece of masonry some eighteen inches square at the end of the arch was able to support the other man who was suffering from severe shock. Mr Wilcox stayed in this position for forty five minutes until the Fire Brigade arrived and Burrows who had become unconscious was brought to the ground by a fireman in a safety belt which Wilcox strapped upon him.

During the period that Mr Wilcox was on the ledge with Burrows he was in considerable danger of falling had the other man kicked out or made any violent movement".

© copyright 1993/MOD reproduced with the permission of the Controller of H.M. S. O.

Charles Wilcox was awarded the Edward Medal and was entered on the roll of George Cross winners in 1971.

Subsequent Career: No information available.

Other heroes

In addition to Birmingham's VC and GC winners many Birmingham men have won other medals such as the Distinguished Service Medal and the Military Medal. Hundreds of thousands of other Birmingham men have fought bravely in Britain's wars. To list let alone describe all examples of such courage would be quite impossible so a few examples must suffice.

Captain Roy Gough DSO

The short life of this brave young man was summed up in the following letter that his commanding officer sent home to his parents Mr and Mrs Gough of Broad Street in Birmingham:

"To the long list of gallant men whom the City of Birmingham has produced and who have died at the front we have now with deep respect to add the name of Captain Roy Gough DSO. The story of this officer's career is almost as beautiful and sad as Mrs Orr-Ewing's tale of a short life. Gough was only nineteen when as a machine gun officer he went to the front with his battalion. His pluck and ability were soon noted and within two months he obtained command of a company. Shortly after his promotion Gough's company had to provide a raiding party for which all volunteered. This raid was costly and many fell. Three times during that night Gough went over the parapet in the face of heavy machine gun and rifle fire and with others helped to bring in the wounded. For this gallant action he was mentioned in despatches. A few months later, in the Somme offensive, he led his company into action. All company officers were either killed or wounded. Gough was desperately wounded but still he cheered on his men and got close to his objective. For this act of devotion he received the Distinguished Service Order. He was sent back to the base hospital and there tended by the cleverest of surgeons and nurses. Here he fought for two months with his usual pluck and cheerfulness for recovery. This alas was denied him and he died at Rouen on October 14th admired by all who knew him. Macaulay I believe describes Hampden as a Christian, a soldier and a gentleman. I can think of no more apt description of Captain Roy Gough".

Corporal Percy Allbut

To quote the "Birmingham Mail" of the 6th August 1915:

"Corporal Percy Allbut, of the 4th Battalion Worcestershire Regiment whose name appears in the foregoing list of recipients of the Distinguished Conduct Medal (the DCM) is the second son of Mr and Mrs Allbut of 106 Summer Road Edgbaston and has recently been promoted sergeant. He has seen fourteen years service. Joining the Royal Welsh Fusiliers he was disappointed at not taking part in the South African war. Eleven years in Burma he there took up telegraphy and attained the position of telegraph master of the military station at Mandalay. He had many exciting experiences in Burma and in April 1912 saved a lady from drowning in the Fort Moat at Mandalay. For this gallant action he received the Vellum Certificate of the Royal Humane Society. Subsequently transferred to the 4th Worcesters stationed at Rangoon he came to England with them when they were ordered home for active service and went out almost immediately to the Dardanelles being one of the landing party. After eight days severe fighting he received a shrapnel wound in the left forearm and was sent to hospital. Quickly recovering he again joined his company and on the 5th of June received a bullet wound in the left hand which necessitated amputation. He was sent home and is now in Graylingwell Hospital Chichester. It is hopeful that he will soon be able to obtain an artificial hand and has expressed a wish to serve as a telegraphist in France".

I have not included details of medal lists for reasons of space.

The Forbes Brothers

The following report appeared in the "Birmingham Mail" on the 13th October 1916:

"The rare distinction of having two sons who are serving in the same branch of the service awarded the Military Cross for conspicious gallantry has fallen to Mr and Mrs J. Webster Forbes of the Hawthorns who have received many letters of congratulation on the fact that Saturday's "London Gazette" contained the notification of the award of the honour to Temporary Second Lieutenant Leslie Frederick Forbes R.F.C. "for conspicious gallantry and ability in attacking hostile machines and bombing railway lines especially on one occasion when he descended to 350 feet in order to accomplish his object".

Lieutenant Forbes who has since been promoted to the rank of Flight Commander and Temporary Captain is 24 years of age and is the second son of Mr and Mrs Webster Forbes. He was educated at the Lickey Hills Schools and Shrewsbury and joined the Shrewsbury School O.T.C. contingent attached to the Shropshire Light Infantry in September 1914. Subsequently he joined the R.F.C. and went out to France in May last as a pilot.

Captain Forbes has lately had rather a thrilling adventure. In the course of an air fight he collided with his opponent at a height of 12,000 feet. The hostile machine fell vertically with a broken wing and Captain Forbes machine fell 9,000 feet before he managed to regain control. He succeeded in flying over 30 miles with an almost uncontrollable machine and eventually crossed the British lines in safety. Unfortunately Captain Forbes sustained a dislocated shoulder and broken arm as the result of this collision and is now in hospital. His youngest brother Captain Ellert W. Forbes R.F.C. had previously been awarded the Military Cross for conspicious gallantry and skill.

Mr and Mrs Forbes eldest son Captain Stanley W. Forbes Royal Warwickshire Regiment (Territorial Force) is also on active service".

Colonel Innes

Lieutenant-Colonel Innes was the commanding officer of the 8th Territorial Battalion of the Royal Warwickshire Regiment. He was killed leading his men over the top on the first day of the Battle of the Somme on the 1st of July 1916. 590 other members of the unit were killed, wounded or captured and twenty thousand British soldiers died that day. The "Birmlngham Mail" gave Lieutenant Colonel Innes the following obituary which was printed on the 5th of July:

"We learn with the deepest regret of the death in action of Lieutenant-Colonel Innes Royal Warwickshire Regiment. The news was received by Mrs Innes today in a letter from Major Townshend.

Colonel Innes succeeded Colonel Ludlow in the command of a Warwickshire Territorial Battalion. He was formerly a Captain in the lst (Birmingham) Volunteer Battalion which he left for the purpose of raising another battalion. Captain Innes who accompanied Colonel Ludlow was given the rank of Major and was made second in command of the battalion in which he became commander on Colonel Ludlow's promotion to the rank of Brigadier-General. Such rapid promotion could have been possible only in the case of a new unit and Colonel Innes progress was almost unique in the Territorial service.

Colonel Innes was the son of the late Mr Innes of Harborne Hill House. He lived at Metchley Abbey, Harborne and was a member of the firm of Innes, Smith and Co. of High Street Birmingham He was an able and fluent public speaker and before the war took a prominent part in the campaign for conscription".

Councillor Henry Lynn Shaw

Three Birmingham city councillors were killed in the First World War. They were Captain Norman Chamberlain, Lieutenant Thomas Silver and Captain Henry Lynn Shaw. Readers who wish to discover more about the tragic deaths of the first two councillors should read my book "Birmingham in the First World War". Concerning Captain Shaw to quote the "Birmingham Post" of the 8th July 1916:

"Captain Henry Lynn Shaw of the Royal Warwickshire Regiment who was killed in action on Monday last was one of the six members of the Birmingham City Council serving with the forces. He was a son of the late Mr Henry Shaw and Mrs Shaw of Birmingham and resided at 2, Pakenham Road, Edgbaston.

Captain Shaw, who was forty three years of age, was the senior partner in the firm of Henry Shaw and Sons, nail manufacturers of Birchall Street. He was associated with the reserve forces in Birmingham for a long period and held a commission in the Volunteers and afterwards in the Territorial force, retiring from the 5th Battalion of the Royal Warwickshire Regiment a few years ago. He was a keen and capable soldier and highly popular with all ranks at Thorp Street. On his retirement he was placed on the reserve of officers and was called up when war broke out. For a time he was placed on recruiting duty at Curzon Hall but he left Birmingham early in 1915 to join a service battalion of the Warwickshire Regiment and accompanied them to the front about nine months ago. He had recently been appointed major, but his promotion had not been gazetted.

Captain Shaw's association with the City Council was very brief. He was nominated as a Liberal Unionist candidate in a bye election in the St Martin's and Deritend Ward in July 1914 and was returned unopposed. Owing to his military duties he was able to attend only two or three meetings of the council and for the same reason was not appointed to any committees.

Captain Shaw married a daughter of Mr George Sydenham and leaves a widow and four young children".

Henri Chatelain

The following passage appeared in the "Birmingham Post" 17th August 1915 and reminds us that not all deaths in war are directly caused by enemy action.

We regret to announce the death on the 19th inst. of M Henri L Chatelain Professor of French in the University of Birmingham. Professor Chatelain joined the French army as a private soon after the outbreak of war and from November to April last he served in the trenches near Soissons. About Easter he was struck down by a dangerous form of illness and he lay for more than two months in a field ambulance just behind the firing line. In June he was moved to a military hospital in Paris where he died on Thursday of last week. He leaves a widow and two children.

Professor Chatelain was among the most distinguished French scholars of his age. Born at St. Quentin in 1877 he studied at the University of Paris under the late Gaston Paris and Professors Thomas, Lanson and Brunot. In 1895 he graduated Bachelier es Lettres; in 1903 he was agrege de l'universite; in January 1908 he gained the Doctorat es lettres (mention tres honourable); and the book which he presented as a thesis "La Mistere de Saint Quentin" was couronne par l'academie des inscriptions et belles lettres and was awarded the prix lagrange. He was a student of wide interests but his special field was the France of the fourteenth and fifteenth centuries upon which he was one of the first authorities.

M. Chatelain was appointed a professor at the Birmingham University in 1908 in succession to Professor Bevenot and he soon proved himself no less able as a teacher scholar. His high ideals of learning, his unsparing devotion to his university work, his gracious manner and his simple dignity of character won for him the respect and affection of both colleagues and pupils and he will be sorely missed. As President of the Cercle Francaise he became known to a wider society in the city and all who cared for the language and the culture of France were stimulated by their contact with him.

My grandfather

My grandfather Thomas Lloyd was born on the 23rd of January 1894. He joined the Territorial Army in 1912 at the age of 18 and served in the South Midland Territorial Royal Garrison Artillery. The commanding officer of this unit was a Major Greg who was a director of the Metropolitan Carriage, Wagon and Finance Company which had been based in Saltley under different names since 1845 and which was and is Britain's leading builder of railway carriages.

At the start of the war the South Midland Territorial RGA were training at Exmouth. They were recalled to Birmingham where my grandfather was formally embodied into the army on the 5th of August and then sent to Swindon where they joined the rest of the 48th South Midland Territorial Division.

The South Midland Territorial RGA stayed with the 48th Division until it went to France where they were detached for service as corps artillery. They first saw action in April 1915 in the Armentieres area. Later they provided covering fire for British attacks at Loos, the Somme, Vimy Ridge, Messines Ridge and Passchendaele. In November 1917 they were sent to Italy where they stayed until the end of the war.

First World War artillery barrages were very heavy indeed. For instance on the 3rd of May 1917 the South Midland men fired more than a thousand shells before breakfast. Heavy casualties were inflicted on the enemy. German accounts describe how a unit of men would be sent to the front line. After a week of heavy shelling less than half the men would still be alive.

The South Midland men suffered heavy casualties. By the end of the war only one officer and 69 men of the unit were men who had been among the six officers and 183 men who had originally formed the unit.

My grandfather was posted to the Second Reserve Brigade on the 21st of November 1918. He was demobilised in February 1919.

My grandfather's reward for serving his country was to be years spent either unemployed or doing casual work while men who had avoided military service by getting exemptions lived well. Eventually he got a job working for Birmingham City Corporation

Tramways. He served in the Home Guard during the Second World War.

When my grandfather was embodied into the army on the 5th of August 1912 he was a healthy teenager who wanted to have some adventure and see the world. By the time he was demobilised he was a broken man of 24. His health never fully recovered from the war and he died on the 17th of February 1953 at the age of 59.

The only medals that my grandfather was awarded were the medals that were given to all soldiers who served in World War One. He stands representative of all those brave men who were never in a position to win the higher awards but whose steady courage saved this country in its hour of need.